GW0514620

This copy of

IN THE STILLNESS OF THE HEART

comes to

Lilly on your 80th.
Birthday

with love from

Every Blessing

Giles & Frank

Copyright © 1995, Eagle Publishing, Guildford, Surrey GU2 5HN

British Library Cataloguing-in-Publication Data. A catalogue record for this book is available from the British Library.

Published by Eagle, an imprint of Inter Publishing Service (IPS) Ltd, St Nicholas House, The Mount, Guildford, Surrey GU2 5HN.

All rights reserved. No part of this publication may be reproduced or transmitted in any form or by any means, electronic or mechanical, including photocopying, recording or any information storage and retrieval system, without either prior permission in writing from the publisher or a licence permitting restricted copying.

In the United Kingdom such licences are issued by the Publishers Licensing Society Ltd, 90 Tottenham Court Road, London W1P 9HE.

Scripture quotations are taken from various translations as follows:

NIV The New International Version

Typeset by Eagle Publishing
Printed by L.E.G.O., Italy
ISBN No 0 86347 161 7

IN THE STILLNESS OF
THE HEART

A COLLECTION OF PRAYERS FROM
THE BIBLE

Guildford, Surrey

The Lord bless you

The LORD bless you
      and keep you;
the LORD make his face shine upon you
      and be gracious to you;
the LORD turn his face towards you
      and give you peace.

           (Numbers 6:24-26)

Reflections
Robert Reid

Praise be to you, O Lord

Praise be to you, O LORD,
       God of our father Israel,
       from everlasting to everlasting.
Yours, O LORD, is the greatness and the power
       and the glory and the majesty and the
       splendour, for everything in heaven and earth
       is yours.
Yours, O LORD, is the kingdom;
       you are exalted as head over all.
Now, our God, we give you thanks,
       and praise your glorious name.
                       (Chronicles 29:11-13)

The Daisy Field
Helen Allingham

Teach me your ways

Show me your ways,
>   O LORD, teach me your paths;
guide me in your truth and teach me,
>   for you are God my Saviour,
>   and my hope is in you all day long.
Remember, O LORD, your great mercy and love,
>   for they are from of old.
Remember not the sins of my youth
>   and my rebellious ways;
according to your love remember me,
>   for you are good, O LORD...

Turn to me and be gracious to me,
>   for I am lonely and afflicted.
The troubles of my heart have multiplied;
>   free me from my anguish.
Look upon my afflictions and my distress
>   and take away all my sins...
Guard my life and rescue me;
>   let me not be put to shame,
>   for I take refuge in you.
May integrity and uprightness protect me,
>   because my hope is in you.

>   (Psalm 25:4-7,16-18,20-21)

A Woodland Scene
Agnes Woodall

Answer me, O Lord

Answer me when I call to you,
     O my righteous God.
Give me relief from my distress;
     be merciful to me and hear my prayer.
I will lie down and sleep in peace,
     for you alone, O LORD,
     make me dwell in safety.
               (Psalm 4:1,8)

Maternal Affection
Harold Harvey

You are my refuge

Hear my cry, O God;
        listen to my prayer.
From the ends of the earth I call to you,
        I call as my heart grows faint;
        lead me to the rock that is higher than I.
For you have been my refuge,
        a strong tower against the foe.
I long to dwell in your tent for ever
        and take refuge in the shelter of your wings.
                                    (Psalm 61:1-4)

A Highland Castle
Alfred de Breanski

Our Father

Our Father which art in heaven,
Hallowed be thy Name,
Thy kingdom come,
Thy will be done, in earth as it is in heaven.
Give us this day our daily bread;
And forgive us our trespasses,
As we forgive those who trespass against us;
And lead us not into temptation,
But deliver us from evil.

(The Book of Common Prayer)

Poor People
Andre Collin

May God equip you

May the God of peace, who through the blood of the
eternal covenant brought back from the dead our Lord
Jesus, that great Shepherd of the sheep, equip you with
everything good for doing his will, and may he work
in us what is pleasing to him, through Jesus Christ, to
whom be glory for ever and ever. Amen.

(Hebrews 13:20-21)

Irises and cow parsley
Charles Robertson

Grow in the knowledge of God

For this reason, since the day we heard about you, we have not stopped praying for you and asking God to fill you with the knowledge of his will through all spiritual wisdom and understanding. And we pray this in order that you may live a life worthy of the Lord and may please him in every way; bearing fruit in every good work, growing in the knowledge of God, being strengthened with all power according to his glorious might so that you may have great endurance and patience, and joyfully giving thanks to the Father.
(Colossians 1:9-12)

The Bluebell Wood
Helen Allingham

Sovereign Lord, Creator

Sovereign LORD, you made the heaven and the earth and the sea, and everything in them. Now, LORD, enable your servants to speak your word with great boldness. Stretch out your hand to heal and to perform miraculous signs and wonders through the name of your holy servant Jesus.

(Acts 4:24, 29-30)

Out of Reach, Daughters of Eve
Sir Frank Dicksee

I will praise your name

I will exalt you, my God the King;
       I will praise your name for ever and ever.
Every day I will praise you
       and extol your name for ever and ever.
Great is the LORD and most worthy of praise;
       his greatness no-one can fathom.
One generation will commend your works to another;
       they will tell of your mighty acts.
They will speak of the glorious splendour of your
       majesty,
       and I will meditate on your wonderful works.
They will tell of the power of your awesome works.
       and I will proclaim your great deeds.
They will celebrate your abundant goodness
       and joyfully sing of your righteousness.
                  (Psalm 145:1-7)

Romping
William Marshall Brown

My soul thirsts for God

As the deer pants for streams of water,
       so my soul pants for you, O God.
My soul thirsts for God, for the living God.
       When can I go and meet with God?...

Why are you so downcast, O my soul?
       Why so disturbed within me?
Put your hope in God,
       for I will yet praise him,
       my Saviour and my God.

                        (Psalm 42:1-2, 5)

Autumn Tints
George Vicat Cole

The Spirit of wisdom

I keep asking that the God of our Lord Jesus Christ, the glorious Father, may give you the Spirit of wisdom and revelation, so that you may know him better. I pray also that the eyes of your heart may be enlightened in order that you may know the hope to which he has called you, the riches of his glorious inheritance in the saints, and his incomparably great power for us who believe.

(Ephesians 1:17-19)

Tea Time
Frank Townhouse Hutchins

Create a pure heart within me

Have mercy on me, O God,
   according to your unfailing love;
according to your great compassion
   blot out my transgressions.
Wash away all my iniquity
   and cleanse me from my sin.

Cleanse me with hyssop, and I shall be clean;
   wash me and I shall be whiter than snow...
Hide your face from my sins
   and blot out all my iniquity.

Create in me a pure heart,O God,
   and renew a steadfast spirit within me.

Do not cast me from your presence
   or take your Holy Spirit from me.
Restore to me the joy of your salvation
   and grant me a willing spirit, to sustain me.
               (Psalm 51:1-2, 7, 9, 10-12)

Winter Breakfast
G. William Quartermaine

You are our father

O, that you would rend the heavens and come down,
      that the mountains would tremble before you!
Since ancient times no-one has heard,
      no ear has perceived,
no eye has seen any God besides you,
      who acts on behalf of those who wait for him.
All of us have become like one who is unclean,
      and all our righteous acts are like filthy rags;
Yet, O Lord, you are our Father.
      We are the clay, you are the potter;
      we are all the work of your hand ...
      do not remember our sins for ever.
                    (Isaiah 64:1,4,6,8)

Landscape
William Hull

Photographic credits

Eagle Publishing is grateful to the copyright holders listed below, and to The Bridgeman Art Library and The Fine Art Photographic Library in particular for their kind permission to reproduce the paintings selected to complement the text.

Cover   *Irises and Cow Parsley*, by Charles Robertson, 1844-91, Guildford Borough Council (Bridgeman).

1.   *Reflections,* by Robert Reid, 1862-1929, Cooley Gallery, Old Lyme, Connecticut (Bridgeman).

2.   *The Daisy Field*, by Helen Allingham 1848-1926 (Eagle).

3.   *A Woodland Scene*, by Agnes M. Goodall, 1913 (Fine Art).

4.   *Maternal Affection*, by Harold Harvey, 1874-1941, courtesy Paisnel Gallery, London SW1 (Fine Art).

5.   *A Highland Castle*, by Alfred de Breanski, 1852-1928, Bourne Gallery (Fine Art).

6.   *Poor People*, by André Collin, c 1862, Musee des Beaux-Arts, Tournai (Credit Giraudon/Bridgeman Art Library).

7.   *Irises and Cow Parsley*, by Charles Robertson, 1844-91, Guildford Borough Council (Bridgeman).

8.   *Out of Reach, Daughters of Eve,* by Sir Frank Dicksee, 1853-1928, Chris Beetles Ltd., London (Bridgeman).

9.   *The Bluebell Wood*, by Helen Allingham, 1848-1926 (Eagle).

10.   *Romping*, by William Marshall Brown, 1863-1936 (Fine Art).

11.   *Autumn Tints*, by George Vicat Cole, R.A. 1833-1893 (Fine Art).

12.   *Tea Time*, by Frank Townhouse Hutchings, c 1869, Cooley Gallery, Old Lyme, Connecticut (Bridgeman).

13.   *Winter Breakfast*, by G. William Quartermaine, 1858-1930 (Fine Art).

14.   *Landscape.* by William Hull, 1820-80, courtesy of the Board of Trustees of the V. & A. (Bridgeman).